KU-560-543

AUSTRIA

Text by

EVELYNE KOLNBERGER

MINERVA

Designed and produced by
ÉDITIONS MINERVA S.A.

Flyleaf: A village in the Tyrol, Heiterwang, close to the German frontier. *Title page:* View of Heiligenblut, at the foot of the Grossglockner.

ISBN: 2-8307-0001-5

Printed in Italy

A WONDERFUL COUNTRY

Austria, this country in the heart of Europe, which for years was also at the centre of Europe politically and culturally, is a radiant country. A country of clear luminous colours: the rich green of the meadows, dotted with spring and summer flowers; the grey mass of the mountains, capped with dazzling white snow and glaciers; the turquoise and green of the delightful lakes; the white, brown and red of the houses with their roofs sloping low towards the ground and their carved wooden balconies bedecked with geraniums; and lastly, the blue of the sky which looks down on all this splendour —blue, at least, when the Austrian baroque angels grant the gift of fine weather...

Austria, a country with its ancient culture, in which the combined currents from the north, south and east blended to create a whole. An old country which has had to face up to problems destined more than once to change the course of the history of Europe. A country for tourists, which has for a long time attracted visitors from neighbouring lands, and continues to draw tourists from far and wide.

Austria, a country which nature has generously endowed with great beauty, and which man has provided with a capital unlike any other. Numerous songs have been written in praise of Vienna, considered by many people to be nothing less than a dream city. Vienna, with its grandiose architecture, its art treasures, its music, its theatres. Vienna, with its incomparable atmosphere and its inhabitants, whose charm and "spice" are famous throughout the world.

Thinking about Austria, and remembering its past, stirs up within us a feeling of pleasure mingled with other emotions: Romanticism in Vienna, the imperial city, the atmosphere of its cafés or "Heurigen", the delicious smell of the Backhendl (pieces of chicken covered in breadcrumbs and deep-fried, and bread and goose- or pork-dripping, Salzburg steeped in music during the Festival Season, the powdery snow and the pleasures of skiing in the Tyrolian mountains, a peaceful little church somewhere in the Mühlviertel, amongst the flower-covered meadows, the clanging of the cow-bells in a mountain pasture and... and so much could be said about all that goes to make up the charm and attraction of Austria.

But the country can also be considered with a realistic, practical eye, and that is what we intend to do now.

From west to east, Austria spreads over a distance of about 580 kms.; its "depth" from north to south is some 270 kms. at its broadest point, in the east; in the west it is reduced to a narrow strip of land enclosed between German, Swiss and Italian territory. With a surface area of about 84,000 square kilometres, Austria is twice the size of Switzerland.

Austria is a mountainous contry. The eastern Alps and their foothills take up about two-thirds of the whole area. Three mountain ranges stretch from west to east. The limestone Alps in the north form the northern range between Lake Constance and Vienna. The central range, the highest made up of primitive rocks, gneiss and granite, stretches from Rätikon, through the Ötztal and Zillertal Alps, the High and Low Tauern, to the Eisenerz. The third range is the limestone Alps of the south. They cover most of the South Tyrol, which now forms part of Italy. They include the Dolomites, the Carnic Alps and the Karawanken.

Between the northern and central Alps flow the Ill, the Inn, the Salzach and the Enns rivers; between the central and the southern Alps, the Drave, the Rienz, the Eisack and the Etsch (the last two now being in Italian territory).

Austria has a population of about 7,460,000, an average of 88 people per square kilometre. The Tyrol is the area with the smallest population, Upper Austria with the highest. One Austrian out of four lives in Vienna. More than 99 % of Austrians speak German, though in Burgenland Hungarian and Croatian are spoken, and south Carinthia is officially bilingual, with German and Slovenian having equal rights. About 89 % of Austrians are Roman Catholic, 6 % Protestant.

Austria is a democratic republic and a federal state, mde up of nine autonomous provinces, the "Länder": Vorarlberg, Tyrol, Salzburg, Upper Austria, Lower Austria, Burgenland, Styria, Carinthia, Vienna. Each "Land" has its Diet and its provincial government. Every four years, the people choose the 165 members of the National Council, and the President of the Republic is elected every six years.

Austria is the land of water: *left,* **the River Sillklamm. The decorated houses are one of its charms:** *right,* **gable of a Viennese house.**

VIENNA IS THE HISTORY OF AUSTRIA.

Vienna is certainly no more Austria than Paris is France, yet it is the heart of Austria. For centuries it was the heart of the Monarchy of the Danube and today it is the heart of the still very young Austrian state. People come there from all over the world. They come as tourists, not having known the town, and most of them leave loving it —captivated by the ancient yet eternally young Vienna. Naturally, Vienna has not only the side over which passing visitors may enthuse, this delightful, lovable side, impressed with the beauty and patina of the years, to which must be added a large measure of warm-heartedness, the memory of painfully sad times, all helped by "Heurigen". Vienna like every other large city, also has its darker side The younger generation of Viennese artists is made up almost entirely of people who criticize Vienna, attacking indiscriminately the defects of the town and its inhabitants, its laxity, its bureaucracy, its out-of-dateness and the excessive number of concessions made to the modern world, which are gradually stifling the heart of the city. No doubt they are

right not to find everything perfect. But it may be said that they too, the most "underprivileged" amongst the Viennese, remain there nevertheless, not leaving for another, better, town, better-organized, better-living. They stay where they are in Vienna, in their neglected town, bustling and wonderful, with all its defects, and its atmosphere, such as can be found nowhere else.

Vienna is a town with a history dating back more than two thousand years. When, in the 1st century B.C., the Romans occupied the Alpine region, they set up a military camp, "Vindobona", on the site where Vienna now stands. Even before that, the Illyrians and the Celts had settled there. At Vindobona a civilian town soon sprang up beside the military camp. Marcus Aurelius lived there for a while and wrote his "Thoughts" there.

The uproar produced by the migration of the different peoples drove out the Romans and also drove back the Huns, Herules, Lombards, Ostrogoths and Avars. They were succeeded by the Slavs and the Magyars. Later came the Bavarians. With the rise to power of the Babenberg dynasty, who

held court at Vienna, the old military camp took on increased importance, having now become a residential town. In 1137, Vienna is mentioned for the first time in archives as being at town. About sixty years later, Walther von der Vogelweide became a poet at the Babenberg Court and sang in praise of the "most pleasant Court of Vienna".

Vienna. *Below:* At noon every day a procession of historical characters appears on this clock, called "Ankeruhr", on a building in the Hoher Markt. *Right:* The Austrian eagle on the gate of a building in Vienna. *Below:* General view of the capital.

As has often been seen in history, good fortune and power could not last for ever for the Babenbergs. After their downfall, the king of Bohemia, Otakar II Premysl, invaded the town. Vienna did not suffer at all from this change of rule. In fact, the town extended its limits, flourished and became ever bigger and more beautiful. Next, the town found itself under the sovereignty of the Hapsburgs, who remained emperors of Austria right up until 1918.

They did not seize power by means of war, as usually happened amongst their neighbours, but rather through peaceful policies, which worked for centuries and may be summed up by this now-famous saying : "Bella gerant alii, tu felix Austria nube" —which may be translated, "Let others make war, you, blessed Austria, make marriages!" It must be admitted, though, that the dynastic marriages did not always lead to the personal happiness of the royal partners! While other nations found themselves rushing into battle, Austria lay on her imperial bed beside the enemy of earlier days, produced some offspring and peace was ensured. What a pity it is that such arrangements are no longer possible today! Perhaps it was not really possible then either. In spite of the Hapsburgs' policy of inter-marriage, new conflicts always arose, causing confusion in the country. During these wars Vienna even fell into the hands of Hungary once. However, when in 1526 the king of Hungary died in the course of his struggle against the Turks, the Hapsburgs gained mastery of Hungary and Bohemia. Vienna was from then on the capital of a great empire. A capital in danger, certainly, for the Turks, who had already conquered a large part of Hungary and the Balkans, twice advanced right up to the walls of Vienna and laid siege to the town, in 1529 and 1683. Both times they had to retreat defeated. Finally, Prince Eugene of Savoy, the "noble knight" put an end to the Moslem threat by his victorious campaigns.

In 1740, a woman succeeded to the Hapsburg throne, the Empress Maria-Theresa, whose reign brought the Austrians not only war with Prussia but also economic and cultural development. Vienna continued to grow and grow, progress was made towards industrialisation and, at the same time, the greatest musicians of classical times produced their immortal masterpieces: Gluck, Haydn, Mozart, Beethoven, Schubert.

The anguish caused by the advance of Napoleon across Europe spread to Austria too. Although Archduke Charles inflicted on Napoleon his first defeat in 1809, at the battle of Aspern, he did not manage to prevent Vienna from being occupied on two occasions. But Vienna won in the end. After Napoleon's downfall in 1814-1815, the European heads of government met at the famous conference of Vienna and there decided upon a new division of Europe. The discussions were fierce but at the same

The hackney-cabs of Vienna are famous the world over. *Left:* A ride in a cab—a pleasure for the countless tourists—and the coachmen have a fund of stories to tell. *Above:* the Volksgarten, laid out in 1820, the oldest public garden in the town. *Below:* Statue of the Emperor Franz I.

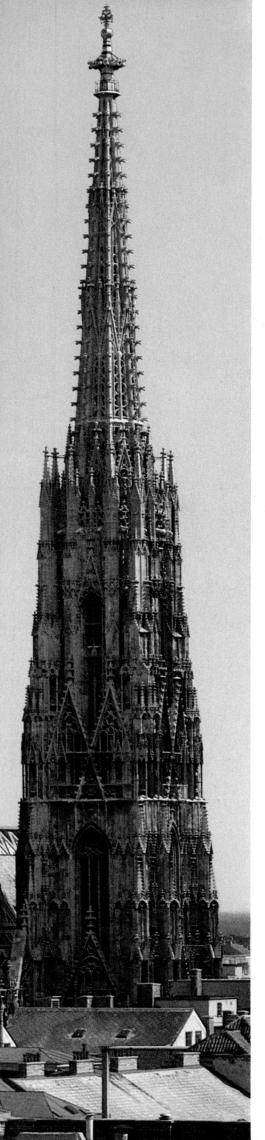

time lavish parties were being given. The Prince of Metternich, the Austrian Chancellor, one of the most able diplomats of his time, directed this kind of ballet danced upon the political scene.

Dissatisfaction was growing, though, amongst the people. Biedermeier's "Healthy Universe" was not, in fact, in such good health as it appears to us today. The Revolution of 1848 released the social tensions of the Monarchy of the Danube. Emperor Ferdinand I. abdicated and Franz-Josef, only eighteen years old, took his place.

With the delightful young Sissi at his side, he became yet another symbolic image of "Happy Austria", over which he ruled for 68 years.

The new era did not halt the progress of Vienna. The Monarchy of the Danube could do nothing to prevent its decline. In 1866 Austria lost the war against Prussia, and had to withdraw from the Confederation of German states and give up Venezia. Vienna, however, flourished as never before and acquired the prestige of a large capital. In 1900, the population passed the one million mark and in 1913, it numbered more than two million— a figure never again reached since that time.

The First World War completely destroyed the Hapsburg empire. The Monarchy of the Danube, problematic yet fascinating state that it was, made up of numerous different peoples, collapsed. Austria became a small state and a republic.

After Hitler had seized power in Germany in 1938, Austria was soon occupied by the National Socialist forces. Hitler himself held a march-past in Vienna and "liberated" the town.

At the end of the war in 1945, a new government was formed and the Republic of Austria was restored. In 1955, the State Treaty was signed.

SIGHTS TO BE SEEN IN VIENNA

A whole volume would be required to describe all the interesting sights of this city, its magnificent churches, palaces, patrician houses, theatres, museums, its broad impressive roads and squares, and its romantic, medieval little winding streets. In these few pages we can only briefly mention some of them and say a few words about the most important and the most outstanding of its numerous very fine buildings.

St. Stephen's Cathedral (Stephansdom), symbol of Vienna and centre of the old town, is a complicated structure, of which the façade dates from the Romanesque period. The huge chancel, divided into three parts, and the nave were built in the 14th century. The two towers of the "Steffel", as the Viennese like to call their familiar and well-loved cathedral, are not identical. The south tower, 137 metres high, was completed in 1433, but the north tower has never been finished.

Left-hand page: **The towers, the high altar and a view of the polychrome roof of the Cathedral of St. Stephen.** *Left:* **The superb spire of the cathedral, built in the 15th century and 137 metres high.** *Below:* **St. Charles' Church with its huge dome and its columns, on which bas-reliefs illustrate the life of St. Charles the Borromean.** *Following pages:* **The facade of the Neue Burg (with statues of Eugene of Savoy and the Archduke Charles on horseback), seen from the Volksgarten.**

St. Stephen's Cathedral is not the oldest church in Vienna. St. Rupert's (Reprechtskirche) and St. Peter's (Peterskirche), which is said to have been founded by Charlemagne but completely altered later, are both older. Amongst the most remarkable Gothic churches, let us mention the Scottish Church (Schottenkirche), the Minorite Church (Minoritenkirche), the Church of St. Michael (Michaelerkirche), the Augustinian Church and Our Lady of the Shore (Maria am Gestade). Their towers still rise up from the old town today and give it its charming medieval look.

The Hofburg, which was for many years the official Residence, stands in a dominating position, together with St. Stephen's Cathedral, in the middle of the old town. Its origins date back to the 13th century. Inside the building, the most remarkable rooms are the imperial apartments of Maria-Theresa, the Chapel and the Imperial Treasury (Schatzkammern), in which are stored all the precious objects acquired by the emperors and kings who lived here over the years. On the

The Hofburg, heart of the capital and the country. Here lived the Emperor. *Left:* Decoration of the gate in wrought iron. *Below:* The very fine "Large Hall" in the Imperial Library, now the National Library. *Right:* The palace at night.

Josefsplatz can be found the Winter Riding School (Winterreitschule), in which the performances given by the Spanish Riding School are held, and the National Library, on the Michaelerplatz, the Michaelertrakt; on the Heldenplatz, the New Palace (Neue Hofburg). In the Capuchins' Church (Kapuzinerkirche), the crypt, called the Kaisergruft (Imperial Vault), can be visited. In one hundred and thirty-eight impressive sarcophaguses lie the members of the House of Hapsburg.

The Graben is a long street in Vienna, along which it is the custom for visitors and inhabitants alike to stroll admiring the lavish displays in the windows of the shops that line their route. When the plague struck the town in 1679, the Emperor Leopold I expressed the wish that a column should be erected, dedicated to the Holy Trinity. At first a wooden column was put up. A few year later it was replaced by the present Plague Column (Pestsäule), a fine piece of baroque work, richly decorated with statues, coats-of-arms and inscriptions. This same

Emperor Leopold also had the Burgtheater built, "die Burg" as it is usually called, which today is still one of the most important theatres in Europe. With an interior hight of thirteen metres and three balconies, the Burgtheater was seen by the people of the time when it was built as a truly amazing building. The Opera House (Staatsoper), on the other hand, is much more recent, built in the middle of the 19th century. It was seriously damaged during the Second World War but the Viennese carefully restored it according to the old plans and, in 1955, the sumptuous building was able to reopen its doors in all its pristine glory.

Much of Vienna consists of a large number of magnificent baroque buildings. Johann Bernhard Fischer von Erlach and Johann Lucas Hildebrandt, the greatest Austrian architects of the baroque style, have made a great contribution to the beauty of the imperial city. With their bright, grandiose style, showing signs of sensitivity in spite of all the power emanating from them, they personify the architecture of late baroque at its zenith, and St. Charles' Church (Karlskirche) represents the very height of creation amongst all the baroque churches in Europe. These same two artists were also responsible for a number of royal palaces, Kinsky Palace, for example, and the Schwarzenberg Palace, the Trautson Palace, and Prince Eugene's Palace. Nevertheless, the most beautiful and most striking achievements of these architects are two castles: Schönbrunn, Fischer's masterpiece, and the Belvedere, the most successful and most popular work by Hildebrandt. Schönbrunn, taking its inspiration from Versailles, is situated in a delightful French garden. It was the summer residence of the Imperial household. It is a fine,

impressive edifice, 180 metres long with a magnificent flight of steps leading up to it. The best view of the harmonious lines of the castle can be seen from the Arbour with its elegant colonnade, which stands on the top of a hill.

Left, top to bottom: The Castle of Schönbrunn, its garden and the Arbour. *Side:* The "Aiglon" on his tomb; it was at Schönbrunn that the son so beloved of Napoleon died and is buried. *Above:* The south side of the castle. *Right and below:* The Castle of the Belvedere, built for Prince Eugene of Savoy.

The Vienna Opera-House and the "Column of the Plague", commemorating the terrible epidemic of the plague which struck the town in 1679. *Right:* The City Hall and the Fine Arts Museum.

THE VIENNESE WALTZ

The Viennese waltz and the Strausses— they are almost synonymous! The Strausses were the great family of the waltz. Johann Strauss Senior produced ballets at Court, was head of music for the 1st civil regiment and travelled all over Europe with his orchestra. He died in 1849, after having collapsed from fatigue on two occasions, for he had not been able to allow himself any rest during the brilliant Carnival of Vienna.

However, even before the father had had to step down from the waltz-king's throne, his son had already been ready for a long time to take his place. The "great" Johann Strauss was born in 1825. At the age of 6 he wrote his first little waltz and, when he had grown up, nobody could stop him taking up a musical career. "Die Gunstwerber", the waltz with which he introduced himself to the Viennese, was greeted with great enthusiasm in the town. From that time on, one success followed another.

Below: **A view of the historic Kärntnerstrasse, and the modern buildings of the United Nations.**

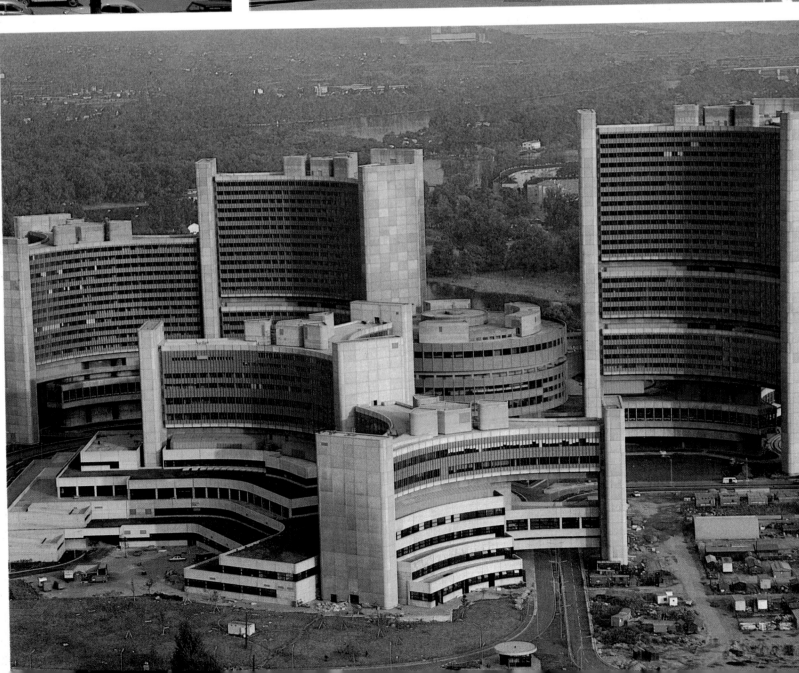

Europe. He was so much appreciated that he could hardly fulfil all his concert engagements, and it was then that a third member of the Strauss family appeared on the scene—his younger brother, Joseph. In fact, he was an engineer and an inventor and only learnt to play the violin as an adult. He then mounted the podium and conducted an orchestra. He was different from Johann —quieter, of a less ebullient temperament than the "Waltz-king", inclined to be melancholic— but he did so well that he soon won the hearts of the Viennese and especially of the women.

As came to be recognized then, he also possessed the famous musical genius. He began to compose. The delightful waltz, "Swallows in a Village" was one of his works. In 1865, he fell seriously ill and died a few years later.

The third brother, Edward, the youngest, then took his turn. He too was very successful, even if not quite as brilliantly so as the other members of the family.

Johann Strauss proved to be indefatigable. "The sounds that I transcribe can be heard in the air in Vienna", he was to say one day. It must have been true. Vienna inspired him, provided him with his inexhaustible imagination and his powers of creation. His magnificent waltzes "Wine, Women and Song", "Tales from the Vienna Woods" and "The Blue Danube" appeared on the scene, as did the operetta "Viennese Blood" and especially "The Bat" (Die Flerdermaus), now famous throughout the world. It was first of all a fiasco in Vienna then, only a few weeks later, conquered Berlin. After this came "A Night in Venice" and "The Hungarian Baron". The ballet "Cinderella" was the last work of this great artist. While he was still working, he fell ill and died on 3rd June 1899.

At the height of his career, Johann Strauss, like his father before him, travelled widely all over

The glory of Vienna has been enhanced by the greatest of composers. *Left, top:* The monument to Mozart and his tomb. *Above:* The house where Schubert was born and one of the houses in which Beethoven lived. The town was in duty bound to raise a statue in memory of the father of the waltz, Johann Strauss (in the Stadtpark; *right*).

COFFEE-HOUSES,
A VIENNESE INSTITUTION

Coffee-houses must have been invented in Vienna, it is often thought, for there is nothing that is more typically Viennese. Yet this is not so; this type of establishment originally appeared in Turkey. The first one was opened in 1540 in Istanbul, formerly called Constantinople. A hundred years later, one was started in Venice, and soon afterwards in London. It was not until 1683 that the first café was opened in Vienna. After their unsuccessful siege of Vienna, the Turks were found to have left behing a few sacks of coffee, and a man called Kolczycki took advantage of this good fortune to found the first café in Vienna. At the beginning of the 19th century, there were already as many cafés in Vienna as grains of sand in the sea. They had become an institution. Much has changed since then, but cafés are still an institution. Each Viennese has his favourite café, where he is known. It was a famous Viennese, Hans Weigl, who explained the position thus. He liked to go to the coffee-house, because there he was neither out nor at home!

At the coffee-house one just drinks coffee. There are a great variety of subtle differences, and a choice ranging from white coffee to a "small black", with more complicated drinks in between, such as the "kleinen Braunen" and the "kleinen Schwarzen", of course, and the "Kaffee verkehr", the "Kapuziner", the "Einspänner", or the mocha

with "Obers", that is, with whipped cream, and many others. No matter what one orders the "Herr Ober" will always bring a glass of water to accompany it. And then one is left in peace, to sit as long as one likes over one's cup of coffee, to talk to one's neighbour or to take one's time reading the newspaper to be found in every coffee-house.

The *Konditorei Demel,* or the *Demel,* represents the elite, so to speak, in coffee-houses. In its beautiful old room, customers are offered all the delights that the Austrian confectioner's art can produce: coffee with pastries and other dainties, and one meets the "best" people in such a place. It was the same a hundred years ago and nothing has changed.

The Viennese author and critic, Friedrich Torberg, made a subtle distinction between ordinary customers and the "regulars" of the *Demel.* He thought that one could only become a "real" customer by succeeding somebody else. It was necessary as a child to be born to a regular customer of the *Demel,* or, better still, to be the grandson or great-grandson of a faithful member of the elite...

Left: **A traditional restaurant in Vienna and the Sacher Hotel, one of the highspots of Viennese life, universally known.** *This page:* **Another of the capital's institutions: the Demel Café, in the Kohlmarkt.**

THE SPANISH RIDING-SCHOOL

Johann Emanuel Fischer von Erlach, the son of Johann Bernhard Fischer von Erlach, to whom Vienna owes many of its most grandiose buildings, also built the "Winterreitschule", the Winter Riding-School. This is the home of the Spanish School, famous throughout the world. Few things have changed in these lofty, bright and harmonious buildings since their construction, except perhaps the number of tourists who today flock to see the "exercises" performed by the Lippizan horses and their riders, who are not content merely to show the great art of horse-riding, the *Haute Ecole* at its best, but they also ensure that the traditions shall be preserved.

The Lippizans are magnificent animals, stallions, almost all of them with white coats, strong, handsome as statues and supremely elegant, though sturdy in appearance. Otto Stoessl, who was a great admirer of the Spanish School, described one of these "exercises": he used poetic, timeless words to depict this superb harmony of understanding between man and animal, this absolute, perfect beauty in controlled movement, which rouses an admiration which takes your breath away. Otto Stoessl died in 1936, but what he said is still valid today. Here, in this hall, combining baroque architecture and equestrian art, the tradition is still maintained. The music blares forth, the dust rises in clouds, the riders' uniforms, deep black, stand out clearly in contrast to the dazzling white of the horses... the carefully elaborated formations, repeated thousands of time, begin...

The riders are slim men with a noble bearing, who, in moments of extreme tension, show themselves to be inflexible in dealing with the tantrums, the excitedness of the stallions, seeming to be firmly fastened into the saddle, solid ore on the liquid ore of the body of their mount. The majestic immobility of the riders emphasizes the wonderful litheness of the horses, which follow the heavily-accentuated notes of the music, trembling with delight, snorting noisily, their legs ready to obey, their heads raised high, drinking in the noise, their manes flying with the lively tossing of their heads, accompanying their movements with a great waving of the tail. The white horses with coats like white silk with a pale sheen, the steely-white horses with the greyish-white sheen, the shiny black horses, are not as thin as race-horses, but sturdy, almost fat, if one looks at their solid legs, their breasts and their necks, but the parts that really support the weight of the body, that is the legs, do so with a maximum of elegance. In these slender columns, so finely formed, on which rests the powerful body, the noble line resulting from the constant exercising ceases to tremble... The greatest power is produced with the greatest elegance...

Another of Vienna's landmarks, The Spanish Riding-School. *Left:* The "Stallburg"—the stables. In the Winter Riding-School, *right:* the public can attend the very fine shows given by the riders during the "exercises".

THE DANUBE, THE PRATER, AND THE WINE

The Danube flows through Vienna. It is part of Vienna. It has for a long time been the living "artery" of Vienna. Yet it is not really blue, as the waltz "The Blue Danube" would have us believe. Perhaps it used to be blue in the good old days...

"At the Prater the trees are blossoming again" are the words of another Viennese song. The Prater, a vast nature park not far from the town centre, with its amusement park, where one can enjoy a ride on the roundabouts, eat sausages and win a few paper roses for one's loved one at the shooting-range, is today, as it was a hundred year ago, a great favourite of the Viennese. Nowadays, as in earlier days, when night falls, young couples embrace under the lilac bushes. And, still now, one gets on to the Great Wheel, this giant, sixty metres in diameter, which completes its circle very slowly, so slowly that one can really enjoy the sight from the top: Vienna by day, in a blaze of sunshine, with its countless roofs of coppery green, its domes and its towers. Vienna by night, with its myriad of twinkling lights; a fairy town, today as in the old imperial days.

And then, let us not forget to mention something which belongs to Vienna alone, the "Heurige", (new wine), with the "Heurigen", little cafés where one drinks the year's wine, the inns and taverns, noisy or peaceful bars where, thanks to a few "Vierterln", one can forget one's everyday problems.

Vienna is surrounded by vinegrowing villages. One is the well-known Grinzing, made too noisy by the invasion of groups of tourists. A second is Sievering, a third Stammersdorf, then Nussdorf. In these "Heurigen", on a fine summer evening, people sit under the chestnut and linden trees at long tables of roughly-cut wood, notabilities and ordinary people mixing with each other; they drink their "Viertel" and bring their picnic, or buy a slice of bread and goose-dripping, a "Liptauer"; they talk and somewhere, perhaps, the "Schrammeln" can be heard playing a tune; or again, perhaps, they sit there, in silence, looking at the pale moon rising in the dusk sky, and the stars awakening one after the other from their day's sleep and, winking and sparkling, taking up their place for the night; they watch the innkeeper as he lights the storm-lamps, and the moths which stun themselves as they flutter around the candle flames...

Left: the vast Prater Park, with its amusements, including the Great Wheel, 60 metres in diameter. *Right-hand page:* the famous village of Grinzing, to whose "Heurigen" (cafés with music) come both Viennese and tourists to enjoy their "Schrampelmusik" in the typically Viennese atmosphere. *Centre:* A panel recalls the "great occasions" of Grinzing!

GRINZINGER
CHRONIK

276 Unter Kaiser PROBUS Beginn des Weinbaus
600 BAYERN im Land - Besiedlung durch Franken
1100 Zur Zeit LEOPOLD III. als Weinort bekannt
1246 Lehensverleihung an Ritter v.GRUENZINGEN
1484 Einfall der Ungarn unter Matthias CORVINUS
1600 Erste Erwähnung des Namens HENGL
1529 1.Türkenbelagerung - Grinzing abgebrannt
1679 Viele Bewohner sterben an der PEST
1683 2.Türkenbelagerung: totale Verwüstung
1713 Wieder PEST und CHOLERA
1809 FRANZOSEN im Ort: Plünderungen, Brände
1827 STELLWAGENLINIE: Innere Stadt-Grinzing
1891 Grinzing kommt zum Stadtgebiet WIEN
1900 Die SCHRAMMELN spielen auf

Donauvater: Father Danube... *Above:* A motor-boat and a barge on the river. *Below:* One of the river's majestic stretches. *Right:* The ruins of a fortress in the little old town of Dürnstein, in Lower Austria, spread out in a rocky setting overlooking the Danube; it is one of the most striking sites in Wachau.

ALONG THE DANUBE

Lower Austria is enclosed by Germany, Czechoslovakia, Burgenland, Styria and Upper Austria. The Danube flows almost across the centre of it, bringing life to the province, a well-loved river, often praised in song, striking as it winds between the vineyards. Vienna is in Lower Austria, and this territory has quite naturally, therefore, always been the cradle of Austria, a province of ancient culture, abounding in art treasures, churches, monasteries, and little old towns and castles.

Klosterneuburg, a little higher up the Danube, is just such a place. The Augustinian Abbey was founded there in 1100 be Leopold III., called the Pious. In the St. Leopold Chapel, the famous reredos of Nicolas de Verdun, created in 1181 by that craftsman from Lorraine to adorn the bishop's throne, represents one of the most important achievements in champlevé enamel of the Middle Ages. The Abbey Church is a remarkable building, transformed in the baroque period, but dating back originally to the 12th century. And the "Klosterneuburger", a wine produced by the vines which

Left: The baroque church of Dürnstein. *Below:* Schönbühel Castle. *Right:* The Danube in Lower Austria. *Below:* Millstatt, one of the most popular holiday resorts in Carinthia.

flourish on the banks of the Danube is wonderfully light and sparkling.

Further upstream, beyond Korneuburg, with its pretty churches, we approach the Wachau. It begins near the twin towns of Krems and Stein, and stretches along the left bank of the Danube as far as Melk. One vinegrowing village follows another and, on the slopes well-exposed to the sun, which look down over the banks of the Danube, the grapes ripen and acquire the sweetness for which they are renowned. Picturesque villages have been built on the terraced hills, and often the church around which they are huddled deserves the visitor's interest. The baroque painter, Martin Johann Schmidt, famous in the History of Art under the name of "Kremser Schmidt", who came from this peaceful, happy region, decorated many churches here —the parish church of Dürnstein, for example, the most attractive of the vinegrowing towns of the Wachau. One cannot pass through the town without drinking a glass or two of "Dürrnsteiner Flohhaxn". But everywhere the wine is delicous, especially in the so-called "Buschenschenken" taverns with a bundle of greenery hung on the door, to show the passer-by that the vintner who lives there presses his own wine.

The Wachau ends at Melk. Let us now cross the Danube and raise our eyes towards the abbey which, powerful and magnificently serene, stands on a promontory above the right bank of the Danube. This splendid baroque edifice was built between 1702 and 1736 by the great architect

Jakob Prandtauer. However, the monastery itself is much older than that. It was founded in 976 as a residence for the House of Babenberg and, from 1089 onwards, has been a Benedictine monastery. The Abbey Church, in which the architecture, sculpture and painting blend with each other so admirably, is one of the most grandiose examples of the baroque style.

Left, top: Castle road at Spitz. *Left and right:* The famous abbey of Melk, one of the most outstanding examples of the flourishing of baroque art in Austria. *Above:* The Spitz vineyards.

CHURCHES, WINES AND SULPHUROUS SPRINGS

A little further on, continuing up the Danube, one comes to the pilgrims' church of Maria Taferl, whose baroque dome was also built by Jakob Prandtauer; the pictures decorating the altar are partly the work of "Kremser Schmidt". The high altar and the richly-carved throne are a delight to see.

From Melk, let us turn almost directly north and we shall arrive at Zwettl. The abbey founded in 1138 and the Abbey Church form part of the most interesting Romano-Gothic building, although the façade is baroque. The cloister, the Chapter House and the Dormitorium are most impressive.

Let us jump now to Bad-Deutsch-Altenburg, down the river from Vienna, known for its sulphur baths. Near this little town stands "Carnuntum", one of the most important Roman settlements on Austrian soil; the objects discovered during digging on the site can be studied at the Caruntinum Museum at Deutsch-Altenburg.

To the south of Vienna, we come to Gumpoldskirchen, a village famous for its vineyards. Many vines grow in this region, but there is no doubt that they do not produce a tenth of the quantity of grapes that would be needed if all the wine sold throughout the world under this label was real "Gumpoldskirchner", a pure, fresh, sweet wine...

The high-society Viennese used to meet at Baden bei Wien, a spa with sulphurous water. Today the little spa has become somewhat quieter, but some of the attraction of its past splendour emanates from it still, a rather old-fashioned antiquated king of charm perhaps, recalling the pleasant leisurely days of the 19th century.

Mayerling, that hunting lodge in which the ill-fated Archduke Rudolph killed his mistress, Maria Vetsera, before committing suicide, is also not far away. A Carmelite convent now stands on the site of these dramatic events.

From Mayerling, one soon finds oneself in the "Vienna Woods", that smiling countryside, with its rolling, wooded hills, a favourite spot with the Viennese for outings. Further on, towards the south, on the Styrian frontier, lies Semmering, a winter sports resort, perched on a sunny slope, protected from the wind, a place reserved not only for winter sports enthusiasts but a delight to all those who like to enjoy the pleasures of nature.

This, then, is Lower Austria, a "Land" with no high mountains and none of the dramatic scenery to be found in some places in the Alps. The countryside here rolls out before the passer-by with no great surprises, none of the breathtaking sights that nature has produced elsewhere. Everything here is soft, serene, peaceful, influenced by art and the presence of vines. And like a fixed star in its midst Vienna the metropolis shines forth.

Left: The Roman remains of Carnuntum; the ornamentation of a stained-glass window in Wiener-Neustadt. *Right:* Two views of a characteristic landscape of Lower Austria.

FROM LINZ TO KREMSMÜNSTER
IN ALL ITS SPLENDOUR.

Linz is the capital of Upper Austria. The Danube crosses it in the north, coming from Passau and flowing towards Vienna. Upper Austria consists of several different types of country: in the north and west, plains rising into hills in some places; in the south, Alpine country with beautiful lakes, murmuring streams and overshadowing mountain massifs.

Like Salzburg, Linz was already a colony in Roman times. It is mentioned as "Lentia" and has had the right to call itself a city since the Middle Ages. Of course, today Linz is a large modern city; however in its ancient nucleus, one can still admire some fine bourgeois houses with their typical arcaded courtyards, dating from the Gothic period and the Renaissance. The 8th century church of St.-Martin, the oldest Austrian church to be preserved in its original form, is most interesting. The old cathedral (Alter Dom) and the castle which now

houses a museum, are also worth a visit.

Near the spot where the Enns river, coming from the south, flows into the Danube, there lies the town of Enns. The most outstanding building here is the basilica of St. Laurent, at Lorch, called in Roman times "Lauriacum". The basilica was erected on the site of a Roman temple and a Paleo-Christian church. Traces of Roman and Middle Ages walls can still be distinguished in an underground sanctuary.

St. Florian's Abbey was built not far from Enns in 1751. The exhibition rooms of the museum and the magnificent abbey church in baroque style are sufficient reward for those who have stopped here on their way through. The composer Anton Bruckner is buried in the crypt of the church.

A little further up the river from Enns, Steyr, although a modern industrial town, has nevertheless kept its Middle Ages and baroque look in the heart of the old town. Beautiful old stately buildings surround the main square, notable amongst them being the 18th century City Hall (Rathaus), the "Bummerlhaus" in Gothic style dating from the 15th century, and the Dominican Church (Dominikanerkirche) in baroque style. The "Innerberger

Stadl", a wheat store in the 17th century, is today used as a museum.

Between Steyr and Wels, almost at the centre of Upper Austria, a stop must be made at Kremsmünster. The Benedictine Abbey was founded in 777; in the 17th century, the architects Carlo Carlone and Jakob Prandtauer designed the Abbey in baroque style. A few parts of the original church, dating from the 13th and 14th centuries, are still preserved —for example, a door in later Romanesque style, and "Gunther's tomb" a Romanesque carved stone.

Top, left: A general view of Linz, capital of Upper Austria. *Left:* The Enns. *Above:* The magnificent baroque gateway to the Abbey of St. Florian, founded in the 11th century. *Right:* The City Hall of Steyr, in rococo style.

BAD HALL AND ISCHL — SPAS WITH GREAT TRADITIONS

Only a few kilometres separate us from Bad Hall, a spa with iodized springs, tucked into pleasant hilly country. For a long time, the country folk living in this area had been struck by the fact that neither their ewes nor their women ever had goitre, which is very frequent in Austria. Thus Jodbad Hall came into being, a spa offering iodized water. There is not actually a spring. The water has to be drawn from deep down by means of pumps. You can swim in the water, drink it, add it to beer —and people do all of these! The dark beer of Bad Hall is also high in iodine content.

Let us move on further south to where the mountains start to rise: Pyhrnbahngebirge, Totes Gebirge and the Dachstein massif. Glaciers on the summits, ice caves, high wild jagged mountains. From Obertraum one can take the teleferic up to the ice-cavern of the Dachstein, and from there one reaches the Krippenstein, a lofty peak from which one has an amazingly good view over the high plateau of the Dachstein, with its everlasting snow, its glaciers and its rocky spurs pointing up into the sky.

Last century, Bad Ischl, the saline spa on the Traun, between two lakes, Lake Traunsee and Lake Gosausee, was the most fashionable spa of the Monarchy of the Danube. In the old days, if one was ill, one went to Ischl, whether a cure would help or not, and in the summer the whole elegant world arranged to meet there. The Emperor Franz-Josef I, who lived for 86 years and spent 83 of his summers at Ischl, was always at the centre of worldly affairs. But it was not only those of rank and renown at the Court who went there regularly year after year; a number of artists and musicians also took up summer residence in this elegant little town, set in the heart of pleasant countryside. Brahms was amongst those who came, so was Bruckner. Johann Strauss composed many of his works at Ischl, and later Lehar wrote his operettas in his magnificent villa there. Leo Fall and Oscar Strauss had connections with the town, and the orchestra of the spa park often played their tunes. And still now the same melodies can be heard whenever, during the season, the orchestra gives one of their concerts. In fact, in the hotels and boarding-houses, the buildings of the good old days, in the tea-rooms and coffee-houses, a little of the old-time atmosphere of the age of Biedermeier is engendered. At Ischl, it seems as if time has stood still. Certainly people no longer go there, as used to be the case, to show themselves off. Now they come for health reasons, to bathe in and drink its saline water.

Above: The pretty old town of Hallstatt, where amazing prehistoric remains are to be found. It has given its name, not only to the lake on which is stands but also to one of the first know civilisations. *Left:* a view of Grundisee. *Right:* Part of the baroque decoration of the Pfarrkirche, at Bad Hall, a particularly outstanding example.

MÜHLVIERTEL, A LAND STEEPED IN MELANCHOLY

Little-known romantic country, situated north of the Danube, near the Czechoslovakian frontier, Mühlviertel does not owe its name so much to the presence there of a number of mills as to the two rivers, the Little Mühl and the Big Mühl, which, coming from over the Czechoslovakian frontier, flow into the Danube. A kind of melancholy hangs over this undulating wooded region, so harsh and gloomy, with a certain starkness in the countryside that contributes to this impression. This might

perhaps be due to the fact that the substratum consists of granite, that hard primitive stone. Farms are often built with blocks of granite. This gives them a massive, menacing appearance, not always very welcoming. They almost seem to be part of the rocky earth, and often look mournful, though proud. The largest amongst them could even be mistaken for little fortresses, squires' residences, if they were not the simple homes of Mühlviertel farmers.

This quiet contemplative country was the home of Adalbert Stifter, who was strongly influenced by

the countryside, which he described in his novels and short stories. Thanks to him, Mühlviertel, virtually unknown to the tourists visiting Austria at that time, found its place in literature. Stifter was also one of the first to take an interest in the forgotten works of art of this region. For example, he recognized the artistic value of the Gothic reredos at Kefermarkt, and fought for its preservation.

Anyone who travels through Mühlviertel province should visit Freistadt, a little medieval town in the north of Mühlviertel, an attractive, sleepy

Little place. But who has ever heard of it?. What used to be the moat around the town is now dried up and overgrown with grass. The houses, built of solid stone, look sturdy and massive, and are closely aligned one beside the other, dwellings with thick walls and high facades. The "Hauptplatz", the main square of the town, is a large open space, with all around it impressive bourgeois buildings in Gothic style, painted in pastel shades.

Mühlviertel lacks something of the bright, almost gay, appeal of the rest of Austria. Its charm is not immediately evident, and certainly does not act upon everyone. It is a question of temperament. However, if you like darker shades you will find yourself attracted by this land of forests, sparkling pools and little towns and villages, all in search of their dreams.

Freistadt. *Left:* The Fountain of the Virgin Mary, on the main square, and the "Böhmertor", an ancient fortified gate; *bottom, left:* Reconstitution of a period interior in the town museum. *Right:* Cross at the top of the Bärnstein with, in the distance, the Moldau. *Below:* This river is the Little Mühl.

THE ENCHANTMENT OF SALZBURG.

Salzburg, which stands on the River Salzach at an altitude of 425 metres, today has a population of about 140,000. It is the capital of the province with the same name, and also a university town. In fact, it is the economic, cultural and tourist centre of the region. It is a very old city. Already before the invasion of the Romans (15 B.C.) the area had been occupied by Celts. Then the Romans founded "Juvavum", which was raised to the rank of "municipium" under the Emperor Claudius, about 50 A.D. In the year 476, the Huns swooped down on the Roman town and destroyed it. St. Rupert, Bishop of Worms, had it rebuilt in 700, this time calling it Salzburg. In 739 Salzburg became a diocese, and in 798 an archbishopric. It had by then become the most powerful ecclesiastical principality in the south of Germany.

Over the centuries —indeed, more than a thousand years— Salzburg has become what it is today: a town where a page of history is turned at every step, and where the proud stately buildings recall to mind generations of Bishop-Princes. Here the music of Mozart, the Middle Ages and the baroque combine in delightful harmony, blending country and city, folklore and a more worldly way of life. The Salzach runs through the middle of the town, separating the old town from the new, but linking them also.

Foreigners visiting Salzburg like to rest their legs at the Tomaselli Café, rich in traditions, or at the "Glockenspiel". The elegant ladies of Salzburg and "initiated" tourists, as we may call them, prefer to sit on the other bank of the Salzach, at the Bazar Café, from which one can enjoy the most beautiful view over the old town.

A street full of life, the most important in the town, the Getreidegasse is a narrow road of shops, where one can buy the traditional costumes of Salzburg and "Mozartkugel" (chocolates with nougat and marzipan, wrapped in silvery-blue paper printed with a portrait of Mozart, although he certainly never knew these delicious sweetmeats); or one can buy antiques, local craftsmen's work, old holy pictures, or bouquets of dried plants, freshly made up, whose special spicy perfume will emanate the whole winter. Or the type of mushroom which is called "Schwammerl" in Austria. Or again records made by the great Karajan. Or clothes signed by the greatest couturiers in the world. Or even cheap trinkets, which also fall to the lot of any town which is invaded all year long by tourists of every race and colour.

Salzburg, festival town, with all the glamour of high society, the prestige of music, the theatre and the ballet. "Jedermann", moving scenes of life and death played on the steps of the cathedral, a tradition and event for ever new, for ever fascinating. "Faust", Mozart's operas. Herbert von Karajan. Pleasure in an art which is enchanting,

Salzburg. *Left:* The famous Mirabell gardens, laid out at the beginning of the 18th century by Fischer von Erlach. *Above:* Salzburg by night, dominated by the fortress of the Hohensalzburg. *Right:* The interior of the cathedral and its square. *Following pages:* General view of the town.

delightful, absorbing. Long evening dresses at the Festival Hall. Dinner following the concert. To see and be seen.

Now for a few remarks about the beauties of Salzburg and the sights to be seen there. There are so many of them that however many times one visits the town, one can always discover something new, magnificent or grandiose.

The Cathedral and the Palace Residence form the heart of Salzburg. The "Domplatz" is a square which has along its east side the façade of the cathedral. The present building was consecrated in 1628, though since as long ago as the 8th century a religious edifice has stood here. The imposing baroque construction, with its massive dome, leaves an impression of grandeur and strength. Once inside the building, the visitor is struck by its vastness and its coldness.

The Palace of the Residence was built between 1598 and 1619 by Wolf Dietrich von Raitneau, one of the most important archbishops of Salzburg. His successors continued his work and decorated the rooms. The two staircases in red marble are superb, with shallow steps that in olden days many visitors went up on horseback. The banqueting halls are much to be admired for the frescos painted on the ceilings and for their harmonious magnificence, never too extravagant.

On the north side of the square stands the Fountain of the Residence, a creation dating from

Salzburg. *This page:* The famous Tomaselli Café and two wrought-iron signs in the Getreidegasse, one of the main streets in old Salzburg. *Right, top:* Examples of regional craftsmanship, and the interior courtyard of a house. *Opposite:* The birthplace of Mozart and his spinet in one of its rooms.

the time of early baroque, built between 1646 and 1661, one of the finest works in the town, to which one always returns. Magnificent horses and magnificent jets, which spurt upwards and stream down, pouring out of the nostrils, flowing through the manes and over the finely carved rumps.

In the "Alter Markt" (Old Market) there stands another fountain, St. Florian's, the statue of St. Florian and the old Court pharmacy, a wonderful rococo building. The house where Mozart was born stands on the left, in the Getreidegasse, and the house where he lived later, on the Makartplatz. The horses' drinking-trough a baroque work on the

Sigmundsplatz; the old Riding-School, housing the "Festival Theatre". Mirabell Castle, built by Lukas von Hildebrandt, in the flower-bedecked Mirabell Gardens, names quickly listed, but each of which marks an architectural period and evokes a particular atmosphere.

St. Peter's, a venerable old basilica built between 1130 and 1143, and restored during the 18th century. It is here that the tomb of St. Rupert, founder of the town and its patron saint, is to be found. Here too —less venerable but all the more enjoyable— the "Stiftskeller" the cellar under the

medieval vaults from which still flows the delicious "Prelates' Wine".

The Church of the Franciscans (Franziskanerkirche), begun in the 13th century, adorned by a reredos by Fischer von Erlach and a Madonna by Michael Pacher. The Collegiate Church (Kollegienkirche) and the Church of the Trinity (Dreifaltigkeitskirche), both built by Fischer von Erlach about 1700. The Church of the Hospital of St. Blaise. The Church of Mülln. And the pilgrims' church of Maria Plain, a charming baroque sanctuary, on the road from Braunau on the Inn, just outside the town.

Let us make our way now up to Hohensalzburg, which stands high above the town. It is much pleasanter to climb up the winding path than to take the fast funicular up to the station at the top. The fortress was built between 1060 and 1088 by Archbishop Gebhard. The present building dates from about 1500. From its towers, corbelling and courtyards there is a magnificent view over the town lying at the foot of the promontory. Inside, superb banqueting halls, including the Royal Hall in late Gothic style, red and blue, with its gold-studded coffered ceiling and its massive columns of red marble; and the wainscoted gilded hall. The huge stove with glazed coloured tiles, of which no two are the same, is the focal point.

The Hohensalzburg is not the only promontory in Salzburg worth visiting. The other hills around the town also have their own particular charm: Mönschsberg, Nonnberg, with its very ancient Benedictine monastery, Kapuzinerberg, each forming an integral part of the town.

The castle residence of Hallbrunn, built by the Archbishop Marcus Sitticus von Hohenems during the 17th century and situated a little outside the town, is another delightful place. The famous fountains gush forth in the grounds, while tourists from all over the world scream and prance around under their unpredictable spray. Also in the grounds, the delightful little "Waldems", a castle built in a month as a surprise for the Duke of Bavaria. In the Hellbrunn zoological gardens, the Alps zoo, live wild beasts brought from all over Europe; the donkeys, sheep and goats lie down with the camels, zebras and monkeys.

Finally, let us mention also the Untersberg, that imposing mountain beloved of the Salzburgers, 1853 metres high, whose summit can be reached on foot or by teleferic. Once at the top one can admire the fine view over the town of Salzburg and beyond to the rest of the province.

Left: One of the doors of the castle of the Hohensalzburg. *Below:* The dance of the "Perchten" in the Valley of Gastein. *Right, top:* Lake Zell, with the mountain of the Kitzsteinhorn behind. *Below:* One of the magnificent stretches of snow in the vicinity of Innsbruck.

THE PROVINCE OF SALZBURG, ITS DISTRACTIONS AND ITS SPORTING FACILITIES

The town of Salzburg and the Salzkammergut are the jewels of the province of Salzburg. However, there are still other places which have contributed to making the "Land" of Salzburg well-known and well-loved throughout Europe. And not only in Europe. Enthusiasts also come from overseas. The splendid alpine mass is popular, either for the majestically dramatic impact of the mountains or, depending on where one is, for the enchanting beauty of landscapes on a smaller, more intimate, scale. In the heart of this delightful country are tucked villages with attractive vast old farms, with their outhouses with flowers, lovingly tended by the womenfolk, tumbling over the edges of the balconies. All this may attract some visitors; others may be drawn there by their interest in sport.

Badgastein, with its luxurious hotels, has for a long time been a popular spa, appreciated also, and especially, in winter by skiers who feel at home in this area. From December to April, it offers them

the most beautiful slopes, covered with powdery snow or névé. There is something for everyone; for the champion skier ideal tracks, for the beginner gentle slopes for practising on, while admiring the breathtaking view of the surrounding summits, on to which they dare not for the moment venture.

Mention must also be made of Saalfelden, Saalbach and Hinterglemm especially, a skiers' paradise of international renown. Zell am See is more sophisticated, a little quieter. In summer, too, one can enjoy a pleasant holiday beside the green waters of its little lake.

Radstätter Tauern and Katschberg are the names of other resorts that have a familiar ring in the ears of skiers and climbers.

The Grossglockner and the Grossvenediger, those two magnificent mountains with their everlasting snowfields and their glaciers, rise on the very edge of the province of Salzburg, but belong equally to the Eastern Tyrol and Carinthia. If the snow slopes of the Grossvenediger are the domain of skilled climbers ready to add to their knowledge of the mountain a good measure of courage, anyone can venture on to the Grossglockner. A well-designed road leads right up to the Pasterze glacier. The splendour of the high Alps, the beauties of the summits just glimpsed by the tourists on their way south, a delightful panorama unfolding before the motorist's eyes.

In the west of the province of Salzburg, let us not forget Kaprun, with its imposing dam standing out against a fine mountainous background. And lastly, the Krimml falls, dropping vertically from a height of 380 metres, a glorious spectacle offered by nature.

Above: The Krimml Falls, with a total height of 380 metres, are reckoned to be amongst the finest in the Alps. *Below:* The Pasterze Glacier, on the Grossglockner. *Right, top:* The Grossvenediger in the Hohe Tauern, with an altitude of 3,674 metres. *Below:* The "Malerwinkel" (painters' corner) near the Grüner Baum Hotel at Badgastein. *Following pages:* View over the spa of Badgastein from the pastures of Bellevue in winter.

THE SALZKAMMERGUT

Salzburg is like a rare pearl, set in the centre of a precious piece of jewellery to catch the eye, surrounded by a multitude of smaller stones which enhance its beauty by the brightness of their radiance.

Amongst these jewels can be counted the blue-green lakes of the Salzkammergut, half of which belong, in fact, to the province of Upper Austria. Set amongst mountains and forests, in delightful tranquillity, they include Traunsee with the elegant holiday resort of Gmunden, Attersee, Mondsee, Obertrumersee, the little lakes of Mattsee, Wallersee, Fuschlsee and Gosauersee, and last of all, because it is the most famous, the operetta lake of St. Wolfgangsee.

When one thinks of St. Wolfgang, a picturesque village, highly-coloured as in a picture-book, which stretches along the bank of the lake of the same name, one can almost hear the sound of operetta music. For it is here that the White Horse Inn of Ralph Benatzky's operetta, known the world over, is to be found. And, since then, from spring to autumn St. Wolfgang has always been seething with activity, joyous, animated and gay.

One cannot esscape from this exuberance at St. Wolfgang from June to October. It is an integral part of the setting. Another speciality of the place, the "Salzburger Nockerln", soufflé omelettes, which are light and sweet, much appreciated by

Above: **The charming castle of Ort, built on an island in Lake Gmunden.** *Left:* **Lake Gosau and,** *right,* **the Attersee, at Steinbach and Burgau** **(bottom).** *Following pages:* **Traunsee.**

connoisseurs. It is wise not to order one when one is alone; it is better to be two, as long as each guest has a good appetite and a good digestion, but the ideal would be to share it between four people, for with a group of friends one can enjoy its savour to the full, without overloading one's stomach. At the "White Horse" and in the nearby inns the "Salzburger Nockerln" arrive on the tables in dozens and, unfortunately, it is not always possible to guarantee their freshness. Times have changed. Mr. Benatzky has been dead a long time. His "White Horse" has been radically altered; from a pleasant, rather antiquated, but well-kept old operetta inn, it has become a mere stopping-place for masses of hurried tourists, who only stay long enough for a quick drink. It is a pity, but what can be done about it? Yet there are, apart from the tourists and the bustling activity, other things to be seen at St. Wolfgang. The pilgrim church from the late Gothic period, situated in the middle of the village, which many people pass without stopping, or even glancing at it, but which contains one of the greatest masterpieces of Austria, à 15th-century reredos by Michael Pacher. The lake is not very large, but picturesque and beautiful: green waters, creeks and on its banks meadows and forests alternate.

Leaving St. Wolfgang and crossing the lake diagonally, one arrives at St. Gilgen, the second most famous resort on the lake. Across the background stretches a panorama of mountains covered in greenery to a fairly high altitude, mountains that are friendly and peaceful rather than grandiose. A steamboat links St. Wolfgang and St. Gilgen, but it is as rewarding to walk round the lake as it is to cross it by boat.

The village of St. Wolfgang, famous for its White Horse Inn. *Above:* Overall view. *Left:* The reredos by Michael Pacher (15th century) is the pride of the church. *Right:* Windows decorated and adorned with flowers, and a door bearing rustic decorations.

ei. Kaffee u. Lebzelterei Wallner

INNSBRUCK

With its 117,000 inhabitants, Innsbruck is the capital of the Tyrol and one of the towns which keeps its place in the heart of anyone who has visited it at one time or another.

In 1239, Innsbruck (the bridge over the Inn) was granted city status. It became the capital of the Tyrol in 1420. The Emperor Maximilian (1493-1519) was particularly fond of the town and chose to live there when he could. It is to this dazzling period that Innsbruck owes some of its superb buildings.

As one walks up the Mària-Theresienstrasse, one can see, rising before the impressive Nordkette range, the mountains of Innsbruck, St. Anne's Column (Anna-Saule), erected in 1706 in memory of the retreat of the Bavarian invaders. The Herzog-Freidrich-Strasse takes us to the heart of the most ancient part of the town, which has preserved its medieval charm right up to the present day. In the year 1500 the Emperor Maximilian had built on to the façade of the Fürstenburg the "Little Gold Roof" (Goldene Dachl) a ceremonial rostrum with a gilded copper roof. The City Hall (Rathaus) with its Belfry (Stadtturm) dates from the 14th century. On the bank of the Inn still stand the remains of the old town walls and the Ottoburg, built in 1494, which used to be an inhabited tower but is now an inn offering a warm welcome to the passer-by.

The "Hofburg", dating originally from the 15th and 16th centuries, was rebuilt in the 18th century by the Empress Maria-Theresa, after the place had suffered serious damage. The "Hofkirche", the church of the Court, contains the Mausoleum of the Emperor Maximilian. This funerary monument is the most important piece of sculpture of Renaissance art in Austria. The black marble sarcophagus stands in the middle of the chancel of the church, surrounded by 28 bronze statues, larger than life-size, representing the most important of the Emperor's ancestors. Some of the statues were designed by Dürer and cast by Peter Vischer.

At the entrance to the church, a monument has been raised to the memory of the Tyrolean freedom fighter, Andreas Hofer, and his faithful companions. Andreas Hofer, a courageous man of the people, now become a legendary figure, was a fierce defender of liberty, who defended his country from 1809, when the Archduke John organised a Tyrolian rising, right to the end. After the defeat of Berg Isel, he continued the struggle with a small group, including the last faithful supporters, although a truce had officially been declared. It was in vain. In 1810 he was put to death at Mantua.

Innsbruck is not only a historical town but can also show a livelier side to its character through its youth. The university, rich in tradition, attracts young people of all nationalities and climbers and skiers arrive in a constant flow. At the 1964 Olympic Games, Innsbruck with the Axamer Lizum and the Berg Isel ski-jump, was the meeting-place of sports enthusiasts from all over the world.

Innsbruck. *Top left:* **The belfry of the old City Hall.** *Below:* **The chancel of the Cathedral of St. James and the "black guards" of the tomb of Maximilian I.** *Right:* **A view of the town, with St. Anne's Column.** *Following pages:* **In the centre of the town, the "Helblinghaus" and the house called "The Little Golden Roof" and some of their outstanding features.**

BETWEEN INNSBRUCK AND THE KAISER-GEBIRGE

The Tyrol offers the most grandiose mountain scenery in Austria. Anyone who likes mountains loves the Tyrol. Some prefer to admire the view from below, following the paths marked out, to go up into the mountain pastures, and are content with that. Others feel the desire to conquer the summits or, in winter, to ski down slopes which are sometimes breathtakingly steep but elsewhere an enjoyable gentle run down. And rare are those who do not enjoy strolling through the numerous pretty little towns of the Tyrol.

Take, for example, the picturesque town of Rattenberg am Inn, with its houses huddled together along narrow winding streets, an important mining settlement in the Middle Ages.

We must especially not, of course, forget Kufstein, the "town on the green Inn" as it is described in many songs; it lies on the frontier between the Tyrol and Bavaria, in a narrow passage, a town bitterly fought over in ancient times. Today Kufstein is a holiday resort much appreciated by tourists; for many people it is also a favourite stopping-place on the holiday route towards, or on the way back from, the south. The town is picturesquely overhung by a 12th-century fortress, high on a rock, which seen from afar lends a certain charm to the scenery. Every day, in memory of the victims of the First World War, a concert is given on the "Heroes' Organ", inaugurated in 1931.

As a backcloth to the town, dominating it, stands the powerful presence of the rugged Wilde Kaiser, one of the most impressive massifs of the Tyrol and the Alps. It is also a massif which fascinates mountaineers. Totenkirchl, Fleischbank, and Ellmauer Halt are familiar names to Austrian and German climbers. These are the mountain faces on which many men and women have learnt and perfected their mountaineering skills, but which have also cost some of them their lives. The "Kaiser" is superb, grandiose —but it selects its victims.

One of the most important tourist centres of the Tyrol is the region of Kitzbühel, the world famous little town. In summer Kitzbühel is a delightfully pleasant place. In winter, during the skiing season, celebrities from the world of sport pour into the town with their followers, and the "jet set" put in an appearance. The "Kitzbühler Horn" and the "Hahnenkamm" are the mountains known and loved by the town's inhabitants. Neither of them has a towering summit, neither can guarantee perfect snow, but there is to be found there a remarkable area for skiing, with marvellous tracks, dozens of ski-lifts and comfortable huts where one can have a drink of that light Tyrolian red wine or perhaps a "Jagertee", the famous dangerous mixture of tea and rum in equal quantities which has been known to turn the head of many a "strong" man and many a good young maid.

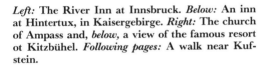

Left: **The River Inn at Innsbruck.** *Below:* **An inn at Hintertux, in Kaisergebirge.** *Right:* **The church of Ampass and,** *below,* **a view of the famous resort ot Kitzbühel.** *Following pages:* **A walk near Kufstein.**

THE LOFTY SUMMITS OF THE EASTERN AND WESTERN TYROL

In order to reach the western part of the Tyrol, which is rather separate from the rest of the province, from Kitzbühel, one must go over the Thurn pass, then cross the territory of the province of Salzburg for some distance before taking the Grossglockner road, or the Felbertauern tunnel, hollowed out of the High Tauern range. The Grossglockner and the Dreiherrenspitze point up into the sky their 3,000-metre-high ice-covered peaks. Backed by the panorama of the Lienzer Dolomiten, the little town of Lienz looks particularly bright and peaceful, contrasting with the surrounding peaks, grandiose and inaccessible. Not far from Lienz there can be seen the remains of the Roman colony of Aguntum .

The Alps of Zillertal and Ötztal—overpowering jagged mountain ranges, cut by deep ravines and with glaciers clinging to their summits, many of the peaks rise to more than 3,500 metres. A paradise for mountaineers, walkers, and skiers, who do not content themselves merely with following the tracks, but can also venture into the virgin powdery snow. Mayrhofen, Hintertux at the foot of the Olperer, Sölden, Obergurgl, Vent, where one can feast one's eyes on the Wildspitze, 3,774 metres high, to mention only a few of the villages scattered over this rugged territory, wild and grandiose.

Between the Zillertal and the Ötztal Alps, the Brenner Pass provides one of the main routes to Italy. In his romantic fashion Goethe courageously made his way along the winding mountain paths. Today a motorway runs over the pass, boldly rising

to the Bridge of Europe, 200 metres high, overlooking the valley of the Sill. And now, let us move over to the western region of the Tyrol. In the upper reaches of the Inn, the Stubaital is magnificent in its stark rugged beauty. No less superb is the Paznauntal, hollowed out by the wild thundering Trisanna. Serfaus, Ischgl and Galtür are villages whose names bring a sparkle of pleasure to the eyes of keen mountaineers and skiers. And, of course, Arlberg, which has for many years been the Mecca of ski enthusiasts. What was said of Kitzbühel applies also, and even more so, to St. Anton and St. Christoph. Here one meets anyone who is anyone, here everyone shows that he can ski and everyone knows how to enjoy himself ostentatiously and expensively. But —and this is the charm of Arlberg and the whole of Austria— it is not necessary to have a sophisticated way of life nor to have a large bank balance. Arlberg can also offer pleasant spots, with the same beauty, ski tracks and entertainment for those who stay in a simple boarding-house and who drink the most humble of red wines instead of champagne.

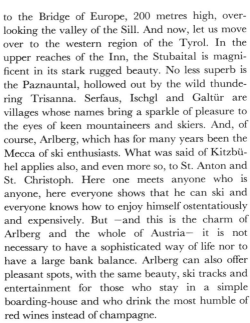

Above: Wenz, at the foot of the Dolomites. *Above:* The sign of a wine-seller, at Rattenberg. *Right:* The Dolomites at Lienz, the lower station of the Zugspitze, the Cistercian Abbey of Stams and a small church in the vicinity of Kufstein.

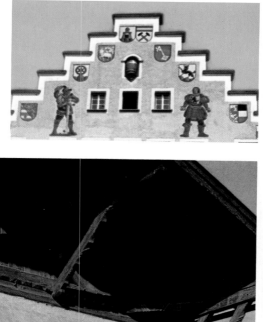

Above: A traditional farm on the Jochberg and some decorated houses, right, a "house of the wine" or "Batzenhäusl", built in 1500 and another one at Flaurling in the Inn Valley, this one built in 1615. *Right:* The village of St. Christoph in Arlberg.

VORARLBERG PROVINCE

Vorarlberg is the most westerly point of Austria, linked to the rest of the country by road and rail over the Arlberg Pass. It was mainly acquired during the 14th and 15th centuries, by means of purchase. Bregenz is now the capital.

Most of the famous Arlberg belongs to Vorarlberg: Arlberg, the skiers' paradise, grandiose and beautiful, on whose perfect slopes, between 1,800 and 2,800 metres in altitude, high society makes its rendez-vous every winter. At Zürs, St. Christoph and Lech the fashionable resorts, at Stuben, a small village which has kept its natural appearance, and at Langen, skiers set off in the powdery snow, or on the icy slopes and, crouching low, rush down the tracks. And the skiers who do not belong to the "jet set" but who are no less fond of Arlberg, come back also year after year. Thus in the snow at least the "great" and the "humble" of our society meet on equal terms.

Bludenz is a pretty little old town. The church of St. Martin, built originally in late Gothic style, contains five interesting baroque altar-screens; Gayenhofen Castle is a fine baroque edifice.

From Bludenz, the Montafon stretches towards

streets. Reaching the banks of the lake one discovers delightful walks along the main quay, treelined avenues and bathing facilities.

The Bavarians, who look over the lake from the other side, have given it the name of the "Bavarian Sea". If, on a murky day, when the mists seem to hang over the water, one casts one's eyes over the lake from Bregenz, one can believe that the Bavarians are right. No bank appears on the horizon. Only the cries of the gulls pierce the silence of infinity.

The Festival of Bregenz, which takes place every summer, is one of its special attractions, the height of the musical and theatrical activities being the "Lake Show". On an artificial island, on a stage raised in the middle of the water, a hundred metres from the shore, scenes from operetta and ballet are enacted. Tenors sing forth their arias. The magic spell is woven, even if sometimes the strong summer breeze wafts the sound of the music away out to sea, or an unfortunately-timed storm suddenly interrupts the performance.

From Mount Pfänder, the mountain of Bregenz, 1,064 metres high, one can enjoy a splendid panorama of the town, the lake and the pleasant province of Vorarlberg.

the south-east, bordered by the Rhine near its source, an attractive Alpine valley, in the shadow of the glaciers of Mount Silvretta and of the mountains of Rätikon, Schesaplana, Madrisa, Piz Buin — magnificent peaks, all more or less 3,000 metres in altitude.

At Feldkirch stands the Schattenburg, the most impressive castle of Vorarlberg. It dates from the 12th century and has now been turned into a museum of folk art. The old town of Feldkirch is still surrounded by a moat and towers, dating back to the Middle Ages. Not far from the gates stand two castles, the Schloss Amberg and the Burg Tosters with its age-old yew trees.

Only a few kilometres separate Feldkirch from Liechtenstein, the tiny little principality which is linked for monetary and customs matters with Switzerland. A paradise for tax-payers, a peaceful little country, green, wooded and mountainous, with its capital Vaduz, which is hardly more than a village.

East of Feldkirch lie the mountains of Bregenzerwald. If we go a little further east, the narrow Vorarlberg already reaches its frontiers. Klein Walsertal forms the frontier region of Germany; politically, it belongs to Austria, economically to Germany.

LAKE CONSTANCE

Lake Constance is a vast lake, shared by Germany, Austria and Switzerland, the largest part being in Germany. Austria possesses only a small area giving access to the lake, in which the town of Bregenz is situated. The whole of the territory around Lake Constance has been steeped in history for many centuries. As far back as the Stone Age, men settled there, and over the years many notable events have taken place on this site.

Bregenz is not a very large town, with a population of only about 25,000, but it is very old. It developed from a Celtic settlement and, in Roman times, under the name of "Brigantum", was a military camp and an important trading centre. The high town is composed of the ancient nucleus of the town, with remains of its 13th century ramparts. Still standing are St. Martin's tower (Martinsturm) and the chapel of the same name (Martinskapelle), built in 1361, with some most interesting frescos. The Vorarlberg Museum in the low town, contains a collection of valuable items illustrating the history of the province from prehistoric times up to the present day.

At Bregenz there are attractive squares, lined with charming old houses, and narrow winding

Left-hand page: **The River Lech, in Arlberg, and the lake of the Silvretta Dam, in the Bielerhöhe.** *Top, left:* **The resort of Lech.** *Bottom left:* **Hall, in the Tyrol.** *Below:* **looking down on Bregenz.**

BURGENLAND

Burgenland is the most easterly part of Austria. It is not to be found on old maps, for under the Austro-Hungarian monarchy of former days no royal province of this name existed. The federal land, called "Burgenland" only came into being after the First World War.

Burgenland is a region of special charm, hardly comparable with the rest of Austria. It is an area which already greatly resembles the Hungarian plains, broad and flat, stretching endlessly to the horizon, which is rare in Austria, land of the Alps. The villages are also much like Hungarian villages: with low houses one beside the other lining the streets for kilometres without there being any sign of a real village; towers with semi-circular arches, wells, geese and black pigs, fields of deep golden-coloured maize at the beginning of the autumn. A peaceful, very romantic part of the country, over which is spread a veil of melancholy.

Of all the particularities of Burgenland, Lake Neusiedl is the most unusual sight to be seen. This huge, flat "puddle" has a depth of between three metres and fifty centimetres, which in itself is extraordinary enough, but, in addition to this, it also happens to be a salt lake right in the heart of a continental region! In the broad belt of reeds that almost entirely surrounds the lake thousands of different species of birds make their nests, among them some that are to be found nowhere else. Lake Neusiedl is, therefore, the Eldorado of ornithologists from all over the world, who eagerly come to study here. Natural reserves ensure that the birds are not disturbed; these reserves can only be entered on foot, or possibly on horseback, for the area around the lake is also a paradise for horse-riders, a real little Austrian puszta. The eastern shore of the lake is especially romantic. Podersdorf, the main summer resort, if one can call it that, Apetlon and Illmitz, delightful little villages situated within the protected zone.

Walnut-trees line the road, and one can stop to enjoy fresh fish from the lake, with a bottle of delicious wine, white and sparkling, or deep red

and heady, which makes one drowsy, but gay... A short gallop takes us to Langen Lacke, a small salt

Left, top, and above: Two views of the pretty Lake Neusiedl, in Burgenland. *Left, bottom and below:* The vinegrowing village of Rust, famous for its storks' nests. *Right:* A mill at Podersdorf.

lake set aglow by the setting sun. Amazing Burgenland, where no feverish activity disturbs the peace and quiet.

Rust is a small, picturesque town, situated on the west bank, a tourist centre and yet, in a way, the end of the world. Low houses, white, yellow and pink, encircled by walls, with interior courtyards, which one enters through a gate set in a semicircular archway. Often a bundle of greenery indicates that the vinegrower sells his own wine. People sit on rough wooden benches, at long tables, and drink the wine served in simple glass jugs; peppers or corn-cobs lie on the whitewashed walls to dry; someone in the party will perhaps play a tune on his violin.

On the tower of the Gothic church, called "the fishermen's church" (Fischerkirche) and containing some fine Romanesque and Gothic mural paintings, storks have built their nests, as they have done for hundreds of years.

At Mörbisch, also situated on the shores of the lake not far from Rust, a festival of operetta takes place every year on a stage constructed on the lake. Romantic moonlight on the silvery waters, a few melodies in waltz-time and the buzzing of mosquitoes...

Eisenstadt is the main town in Burgenland, a pleasant little town set amongst vineyards, containing many reminders of Joseph Haydn who lived for some years at Esterhazy Castle, as Master of the Chapel. The present magnificent elaborately-decorated castle was built in 1672 and stands in beautiful grounds.

In the town itself, a visit must be made to the museum and the underground Church of Calvary, in which Haydn is buried. He was born not far from here, at Rohrau in Lower Austria, already at that time marked by the melancholy nature of Burgenland.

In the village of St. Margarethen contemporary artists have arranged an open-air museum of sculpture in a Roman quarry. A delightful contrast between the past and modern art.

In its southern part, Burgenland really deserves its name (land of castles). On gentle slopes of vine-clad hills stand castles and fortifications, standing out against the sky in the bright light of this region. One of them is Bernstein Castle (Bernstein = yellow amber), so called because of the amber found here, which has nothing to do with the real yellow translucent amber from the Baltic Sea, but is a

greenish schiste. There is a connection, however, with real amber. The ancient amber route did, indeed, pass through Burgenland, linking the Baltic Sea with the Roman Empire. There are also castles at Drassburg and Güssing. Kobersdorf was in former days a manor house surrounded by water. Forchenstein, without any doubt the finest of all the castles, built in about 1300 and restored during the 17th century, contains an outstanding collection of weapons.

Finally, just a word about one of the villages, insignificant certainly but which deserves a mention because one of the great musicians of the 19th century was born there: Franz Liszt. The village is called Raiding.

Austria, like Alsace in France, is the land of storks. *Above:* A storks' nest at Rust. *Below:* The Castle of the Princes Esterhazy, at Eisenstadt. *Right:* Houses typical of Burgenland, at Mörbisch.

Left-hand page: A view of the famous Puszta and the house where Franz Liszt was born, at Raiding. *Above:* A caravan holiday in Burgenland. *Left:* Storks again, faithful to this region. *Below:* The wild romantic setting of the fortress of Forchtenstein.

GREEN STYRIA

The name "Green borderland" is given to this charming region where forests and gently-sloping mountains alternate with fields of corn, maize and pumpkins, and over which blows a fresh wind from Dachstein and its glaciers or a gentle breeze from the south, good for the vines, which gives the wine its special warmth and its particular bouquet.

Graz is the capital of Styria, a university town, rich in tradition, delightfully charming. The medieval clock-tower on the Schlossberg promontory, overlooking the town from a height of about a hundred metres, is its symbolic image. In this tower, built in 1598, hangs the largest bell in Styria, "Liesl", weighing more than eight tons. The old fortress of Schlossberg was dismantled in 1809 but the castle museum contains a model of the old fortification. In the casemates a small open-air theatre has been constructed, on the stage of which takes place each year the "Graz Summer Festival". But throughout the year Graz is famous for the many good plays performed in its politically-involved theatre. Graz is essentially a town with an active cultural life. It is also a lovely ancient town.

The Gothic cathedral (Dom), which dates from 1462, is well worth visiting, especially for its frescos and the "Italian chests" that it houses. Just beside it stands the Mausoleum of Emperor Ferdinand II, a baroque construction, built from sketched designs by Fischer von Erlach.

The arsenal is an especially remarkable building. It was put up to house the weapons stocked at Graz, as the main arms deposit for the whole of Austria used to be here in Graz. As they were needed, the arms were sent from Graz to the different fortresses and castles defending the frontiers to the south and the east, and also sent to the interior of the country, to the lords, so that they might ensure that their vassals had all the necessary equipment. The arsenal is still there today and contains all the 16th- and 17th-century arms — almost 30,000 weapons— the largest collection of medieval arms in the world.

The "Joanneum" is the provincial museum of Styria, and the most extensive library in Austria, with some 500,000 volumes! We owe its foundation, as well as that of most of the other remarkable buildings in the town, to Archduke John who, in 1811, chose to take up residence in Styria and to make it a "model province", as much for its prosperity as for its culture and education.

Graz. *Left:* A view of the town from a terrace of the Schlossberg, and two decorated houses. *Right, top:* The roofs of the town; a wrought-iron well. *Right:* Another well, in the courtyard of the Landhaus; the Clock Tower, symbol of the town, whose four sides each bear a huge face, surmounted by a wooden gallery.

THE GRAZING-LANDS
OF THE LIPPIZANS AT PIBER

The stables where the Lippizan horses, made famous by the Spanish Riding-School in Vienna, are bred are to be found at Piber, not far from Graz.

The breeding of Lippizans began in 1580 in the Austrian Court stables at Lippiza, near Trieste. It is there that this breed was raised to perfection, superb powerful horses with shining white coats, strong but elegant, with a mixture of Arab, Spanish and Italian blood. For centuries, the Lippizans came from Lippiza, as their name indicates. However, after the division of Austria at the end of the First World War the stables were on what was destined to become Italian territory. From the half of the stock that Austria still possessed, new stables were built up after the war at Piber in Styria, where there had been a military stable since 1798.

For the next two decades, until the Second World War, the white horses were bred here, showing the same qualities as before at Lippiza. In 1942, the stables were closed, and the breeding mares were put into safety in the Forest of Bohemia and in Upper Austria, until it was safe to bring them back to Piber in 1947.

As in the olden days, the six famous dynasties of stallions are represented there: Conversano, Favory, Maestuoso, Napolitano, Pluto and Siglavy. If necessary for reproduction, stallions from the Riding-School in Vienna are sent for.

However, Graz and Piber are not the whole of Styria. It is a province endowed with great beau-

ies, on both a large and small scale, a land of forests and vineyards, in which one is constantly coming upon cultural treasures from the past. Delightful little towns invite the visitor to stay a while. Bruck an der Mur, with the Kornmesserhaus, a superb Gothic building, Eisernerz, with its Renaissance Fountain and the Erzberg, whose ore has been exploited on the surface for more than 2,000 years. The interesting Church of St. Oswald at Eisenerz should also be mentioned. At Judenburg, the 15th-century wood-carvings are admirable. At Seggau, Roman remains and other excavations recall the Roman "Flavia Solva". The Romanesque basilica of Seckau, dating from the 12th century is one of the most outstanding masterpieces in Styria. Another artistic achievement, Stainz Abbey, founded in 1230, an imposing edifice in baroque style. Lastly, Vorau, with its 12th-century abbey, of which the library, with its collection of manuscripts, draw the highest praise from bibliophiles everywhere.

A trip through Styria to see only its art treasures would be a most enjoyable undertaking. There would be churches, castles and little towns to admire, and in between times, one could savour the quality of the wine. One would stand amazed before the imposing fortresses, Altenburg, Festenburg and Riegersburg, with its fine interior decoration and its seven gates. And everywhere the radiant fruitful countryside, luxuriantly green. Ideal country for pleasurable relaxation.

Left: The resort of Ramsau, at the south of the Dachstein massif. A statue of the Archduke John, who was in love with a countrywoman from the region. *Right:* Murau, capital of the Murtal, in Styria. *Below:* A view of the famous stables of Piber, from which the famous Lippizans come. *Following pages:* The green paddocks of Piber.

PILGRIMAGE TO MARIAZELL

About the middle of the 12th century, Abbot Otakar, of the monastery of St. Lambrecht, sent a monk to the region surrounding what is now Mariazell, in Styria, to evangelize the still primitive and pagan population. The monk thus set off on horseback alone, and when he came to a place that pleased him he set up his camp. In a linden forest, he carved a statue of the Virgin Mary, set it on a tree stump, then built a simple hermitage nearby. Little by little the men who lived in the surrounding forests drew near. The monk decided to remain amongst them to instruct them in the Christian faith and to teach them to live in the fear of God.

One fine day, the little statue of the Virgin Mary that the monk had carved with his clumsy hands turned out to be a miraculous image. Prayers made at the foot of the "Magna Mater Austriae" were answered.

The fame of the new miraculous image spread rapidly. Soon, on horseback or on foot, the first pilgrims crossed the almost impassable mountainous region, to reach the little statue. Amongst them was the margrave Heinrich von Mähren, who, following his miraculous recovery from a painful disease, had the first chapel built on this hallowed spot. After a victorious campaign, King Louis of Hungary, in gratitude, had a further church built above the earlier chapel. Today both the chapel and the Gothic church are still visible, forming part of the magnificent basilica. The central tower is Gothic, flanked by two bulbous baroque towers — the unique synthesis of Austrian architecture at the end of the Middle Ages and the baroque period.

As pious tradition at least has it, the very ancient miraculous image of the "Magna Mater Austriae", carved in linden wood, still stands on the very spot where in the 12th century the monk originally placed it.

For centuries Mariazell was the religious centre of the Austro-Hungarian monarchy. And it is still today a centre to which people come in large groups, from far and wide. Many of them are merely curious, or holidaymakers —Mariazell has not, any more than other famous places of pilgrimage, been spared the inevitable irreverent activities and the bad taste—others take a serious interest in the art treasures in the church. As in olden days, however, many are believers who hope for the intercession of the miraculous Virgin. Pilgrims used to come on foot or on horseback, spending days or even weeks on the road, suffering hardship and facing danger. Nowadays they travel in comfortable coaches. The customs have changed but the prayers remain the same.

Top left: View of Mariazell, the most visited place of pilgrimage in Austria. *Below:* The basilica, the work of the architect Dominic Sciassia. *Right:* Statue of the Virgin Mary, patron of the place, and an unusual view of one of the bulbous towers of the sanctuary.

CARINTHIA

Carinthia (in German: Kärnten), which has given its name to the smart "Kärtnerstrasse" in Vienna, is situated in the south-east of Austria. It is an especially sunny federal province, which borders on Yugoslavia and Italy, and whose mild climate is much appreciated as a real blessing offered by nature. Carinthia enjoys 2,000 hours of sunshine a year, as the travél brochures claim. It has 1980 lakes, large and small, partly-ruined fortresses and well-preserved castles, mountains and springs, churches and comfortable inns where one can taste the good light wine.

The highest mountain in Carinthia and, indeed, in the whole of Austria, is the Grossglockner, which stands at the place where the provinces of Salzburg, the Tyrol and Carinthia meet. The High Tauern belong to Carinthia, as do the Karawanken, towering over peaceful lakes. The River Drave crosses Carinthia from east to west, and the three main towns of this province all stand on its banks: its capital, Klagenfurt, Villach and Spittal am der Drau.

Klagenfurt's emblem is the dragon, which adorns the fountain (Lindwurmbrunnen) of the Neuere Platz. The Landhaus, the former palace of the States of Carinthia, the cathedral and the residence of the Bishop-Princes are some of the outstanding buildings. When night falls, it is good to climb to the top of the tower of the Parish Church (Pfarrkirche), which has a gallery round it. There is a magnificent view over the Karawanken, glowing pink in the light of the setting sun, and over the sparkling lakes, which at this time of night, look as silvery as mother-of-pearl.

At the Carinthian Regional Museum, the lapidary fragments from the Roman "Virunum", "Teurnia" and the Magdalensberg are on show, reminders of the early history of the country during the Celtic and Roman occupations.

Not far away from here, to the north of Klagenfurt, is the Magdalensberg, the mountain on which traces of the 1st-century Celtic and Roman occupations were found during excavations. Most of what the diggings have brought to light comes from the circle of Roman culture, although the mark left by the Celts is appreciable. The marathon around four mountains, one of which is the Magdalensberg, which still took place every year during the 19th century, on the second Friday after Easter, is certainly of Celtic origin.

Even nearer to Klagenfurt than the Magdalensberg is the place of pilgrimage of Maria Saal. It was founded as early as the 8th century. In the 15th century, the twin-towered Gothic church was built, the interior decorated with a reredos with volets, richly-carved and very fine, as well as frescos of great artistic value.

Left: Detail of a rustic cottage at Maria Saal; the church, a place of pilgrimage. *Right:* Aerial view of Friesach.

HOCHOSTERWITZ, THE PICTURE-BOOK CASTLE

Such is the emblem of Carinthia and, moreover, the most beautifully situated castle in the whole of Austria —Hochosterwitz Castle, which used to be called "Astarvizza" in the olden days. During the attack by the Turks, it welcomed thousands of men, offered them protection and saved their lives. Looking through old history books, one learns that already as long ago as the year 1200, there was a fortress bearing the name of Osterwitz.

The present fortress, with its 14 gates, was built in the 16th century by a pious Protestant. He was called Georg von Khevenmüller and the castle still belongs to his descendants. The castle of Hochosterwitz can be seen from afar, standing at a height of 150 metres on a limestone rock, a magnificent fortress, a grandiose construction with its 14 gateways forming towers — certainly the most beautiful and most fascinating castle that Austria has to offer. The way up the fortified approach through the 14 gateways is unique. Each gate has its own courtyard, a name of its own, and is part of a cunning system of defence. Each has its own history, sculptures and inscriptions.

In the 13th century, Duke Bernhard of Carinthia appointed the lords of Hochosterwitz as cup-bearers. He was a man who enjoyed life, and a patron of poets and singers. He summoned to his Court the famous Minnesänger Walther von der Vogelweide; or perhaps the wandering singer found his own way to the castle of Hochosterwitz.

The visitor of today should be able to imagine himself in the past as he climbs the steep approach road, passing through the 14 gates, and visiting the castle of Hochosterwitz with its strong walls, its towers and its residential apartments. Perhaps this faculty for dreaming, these reminiscences of the past, will be facilitated when he sits down in the castle tavern. The massive tables are set up in the old courtyard of the castle, surrounded by rough wooden benches, amongst the living setting of the past. One drinks one's "Vierterl" of Carinthian wine, then perhaps a second, and a third, and later on, a fourth, and anyone who has a reflective, imaginative turn of mind will hear the clear clinking of swords striking on the shields of those taking part in the tournament, or the sound of caparisoned horses pawing the ground... and he may even see the frail bewitching mistress of the castle coming towards him with a smile...

Above: **The imposing castle of Hochosterwitz, with its vast approach.** *Left:* **an ex-voto, such as are often to be found along the edge of country roads.** *Right:* **In the centre of Klagenfurt, the Landhaus, an old palace of the States of Carinthia, and the church.**

THE FASCINATING CITIES
OF CARINTHIA

If one runs one's mind over the different federal provinces in Austria, trite phrases spring to the lips and one has difficulty in avoiding repeating oneself. In Carinthia, too, the splendour of the natural attributes, and the beauties that European civilization and history have created, from an incomparable sensual and intellectual unity, a unity in which the two constituent elements complete each other. It is only together that they reach their zenith.

From the castle of Hochosterwitz it is only a short distance to the valley of Gurk, a picturesque wide river valley, in which is situated the most important building in the history of Carinthian art, and especially one of the most interesting churches in Central Europe: the Romanesque Cathedral of Gurk. It was founded between 1140 and 1200. Outside, seen from afar with its simple light-green cupolas on white walls, it appears familiar rather than grandiose or even imposing. Inside, however, unique art treasures are to be found: in the wertern part of the gallery, the most important Romanesque frescos in any German-speaking country, the "Kingdom of Heaven", the Episcopal Chapel, with its strong, luminous colours, and the outstanding crypt, supported by a real forest of columns — about a hundred of them.

Let us return now in the direction of the Drave to reach Villach. As long ago as the most distant of prehistoric days, at the time of Hallstadt, the region around Villach was populated, and during Roman times a large colony grew up there "Sanctium". Even at this time the beneficial effect of the thermal springs was known, and still now they make Warmbad Villach a very well-frequented spa. Thanks to the continuation of this traditional activity, Villach is able to offer high-quality gastronomy and many different distractions. But it is also a charming little town. Fine Renaissance buildings stand round the main square, and the Parish Church in Gothic style is worth a visit its 15th-century frescos.

Further on towards the north-west, on the banks of the Dave, is Spittal, a small town with only 1,200 inhabitants. The houses have superb facades and pleasant arcaded courtyards provide a delightful atmosphere of peace and quiet. Spittal can also boast Porcia Castle, built between 1529 and 1602, one of the most magnificent Renaissance castles in Austria, and one of the most exciting from an artistic point of view.

Anyone who is interested in the remains of prehistoric civilization should continue a further few kilometres in the direction of St. Peter im Holz, which stands on the site of the ancient Celtic "Teurnia". The excavations are worth a visit.

Left: Roman bas-relief from Virunum in Carinthia. *Below:* The former City Hall, today Rosenberg Palace, at Klagenfurt. *Right:* The countryside in the Villacher pastures. *Below:* Interior courtyard of the Porcia Castle, at Spittal.

LAKE COUNTRY

Around the little towns of Carinthia, north and south of the Drave, stretches the Seenplatte, an ideal holidays area, still typically Austrian: blue waters, green meadows, dotted with flowers of every hue, welcoming mountains in the background, solidly-built farms, a rustic softness; but over all this shines an almost Italian sunshine, a softer light, warmer than in the regions of the provinces situated further north, which are much rougher.

The lakes called Millstadt, Ossiach, Worth, Faak, Weissensee and Klopeiner are dotted about in gently-undulating hilly country, in the heart of dense forests and surrounded by vast cornfields, which in summer shine with a deep golden radiance. Serenity and softness are the main characteristics of this region, which has no spectacular, dramatic aspect, where apples, pears and grapes ripen earlier than anywhere else, and where, on clear days, the Karawanken seem to smile with thier "rosy cheeks", as it is said in ancient poems. Here one can bathe in the warm waters of the lakes, and walk without any over-strenuous effort, enjoying the pleasures of nature.

It is not thanks to any miracle that Carinthia is one of the most popular tourist areas in Austria.

The enchantingly pretty villages round the lakes are popular with a sophisticated clientele. Luxury hotels stand side by side with the old farms, and in the summer the farmers withdraw with their beds to their lofts so as to be able to rent their rooms to tourists.

Velden and Pörtschach, on Lake Worth, open their doors to the "jet set". Sports cars, head to tail, block the narrow streets. Entertainment of all kinds is available all round the clock. There is even a casino. A little of the silence and the peaceful life of earlier days can still be found at Maria Wörth, the little peninsula situated on the south bank of the lake, where the oldest Christian colony in Carinthia once stood. In the "Winterkirche" (a smal sanctuary consecrated in 1115 and restored in 1355), interesting remains of Romanesque frescos have been preserved and the Parish Church deserves a mention also, because of its Romanesque door and its fine ornate high altar in baroque style. One event not to be missed: a candlelight procession which takes place each year at Maria Wörth on the 15th August, the Day of the Assumption.

That, then, is Carinthia. But Carinthia is much more than this! Countless little-known towns and villages, as well as tiny lakes, monasteries and castles, some of which house remarkable artistic treasures. Others contain no masterpieces, nothing that could appear in "Baedecker". They are simply beautiful and pleasant. In the north and south of the province rise high mountains. The Grossglockner is the highest and shines with and the glow of its superb glacier, the Pasterze. But the Ankogel and the Almspitze, with their extensive glaciers, are also higher than 3,000 metres.

Here, then, in Carinthia, in the south-east, we end our journey through Austria. A journey that one would always like to do again, in detail, region by region, preferably idling along without hurrying, without a thought but that of enjoying the beauty around. What is to be our conclusion? "Auf Wiedersehen", farewell, goodbye? But no, we are in Austria, so we must say: "Servus"!

Left: Living folklore—popular music and country dances. *Above:* A view of Millstadt, on the lake of the same name. *Right:* View over Maria Wörth. *Last page:* One of the beautiful churches, so characteristic of the Tyrol, (at Lüblfing).

Abbé/Vloo 68a, 86a, 87a, b – Anatol/Zefa 15c, 16d, 18d
– Aotani/Atlas 73b – Barrault/Vloo 28b – Berenger/P
14a, b, 25c, 45c, 57b – Berne/fotogram 45b – Buchner/Z
fa 70a – Carle/Zefa 19, 86b – CASH/Pix 45e, 49b, 92b –
Colour Library Int./LSP Endpapers, 30b, 72a – Corte/Vlo
15b – Damm/Zefa 9a, 20b, 25a, e, 76b, 81d, 95d – D
vis/Feature Pix/Vloo 6b – Diana/Fiorepress 46a – Eige
/Zefa 24b –Essem/LSP 58a, 70b, 80a – Fiore/Fiorepress
4, 5b, 12a, 20c, 31b, 34a, 93a – Fitz/ÖFVW 83a – G
ugez/fotogram 14d – Goebel/Zefa 50, 73a – Gontscharo
/Pix 59 – Gottfried/ÖFVW 47a, 78b – Grossauer/Ze
46b, 74a, 76a, 79b – Grünert/ÖFVW 69a, 82b – Hauc
/Zefa 9b – Hoppichler/ÖFVW 71 – Inko/Zefa 49a – Jun
26a, c, 38a, b, c, 39a, b, 42, 90b – Kanus/Vloo 54
Kerth/Zefa 17a, 27, 31a, 33a, b – Knight/Vloo 8a, 25b
Kurverwaltung Millstatt/ÖFVW 29b – Lamm/ÖFVW 82
– Len Sirman Press 44b, c, 56a, 96 – Mairani/Neri 34
52a, 58c – Mangiavacca/Neri 8b, 41b, 69b, 70c, d – M
ngiavacca/Vloo 14c, 64b, 66 – Markowitsch/ÖFVW 18
41c, 44a, 47b, 48a, 75b, 78a – Masser/Zefa 77 – Massau
/Vloo 23b – Messerschmidt/Vloo 7b, 12b, 13, 16a, b
Messerschmidt/Zefa 15a – Mischler/Vloo 21b – Mistle
/Vloo 21a – Müller/Zefa 72b – nt/Zefa 64a – ÖFVW 20
– Peuriot/Pix 10, 16c, 28a, 30a, 35, 36a, b, 53b, 68c, d –
Phillips/Zefa 1, 18a, 90a – Ploquin/Pix 5a, 6a, 7a, 17b, 22a
b, 37, 52b, 53a, 58b, 65a, 68b, 75a, 84, 93b – Popularis/LS
24a – Prenzel/LSP 18c – Pr/Ricciarini 8c, 45a, d, 56b, 57a
62, 63, 80b, 81a, b, 88a, 92a – Puttati/Vloo 65b – Ro
senfeld/Zefa 74b, 94a – Simoner/ÖFVW : Unedi 25d, 32
– Starfoto/Zefa 26b – Thonig/Zefa 40, 41a – Trenkwalder
/Zefa 89, 91, 94b – Valarcher/Atlas 60 – Viollet 2, 29a
34b – Viollon/Zefa 48b – Volfsberger/Zefa 18e, 73c, 79c
95a.